SCIENTOLOGY
Improving Life in a Troubled World

Founded and developed by L. Ron Hubbard, Scientology is an applied religious philosophy which offers an exact route through which anyone can regain the truth and simplicity of his spiritual self.

Scientology consists of specific axioms that define the underlying causes and principles of existence and a vast area of observations in the humanities, a philosophic body that literally applies to the entirety of life.

This broad body of knowledge resulted in two applications of the subject: first, a technology for man to increase his spiritual awareness and attain the freedom sought by many great philosophic teachings; and, second, a great number of fundamental principles men can use to improve their lives. In fact, in this second application, Scientology offers nothing less than practical methods to better *every* aspect of our existence—means to create new ways of life. And from this comes the subject matter you are about to read.

Compiled from the writings of L. Ron Hubbard, the data presented here is but one of the tools which can be found in *The Scientology Handbook*. A comprehensive guide, the handbook contains numerous applications of Scientology which can be used to improve many other areas of life.

In this booklet, the editors have augmented the data with a short introduction, practical exercises and examples of successful application.

Courses to increase your understanding and further materials to broaden your knowledge are available at your nearest Scientology church or mission, listed at the back of this booklet.

Many new phenomena about man and life are described in Scientology, and so you may encounter terms in these pages you are not familiar with. These are described the first time they appear and in the glossary at the back of the booklet.

Scientology is for use. It is a practical philosophy, something one *does*. Using this data, you *can* change conditions.

Millions of people who want to do something about the conditions they see around them have applied this knowledge. They know that life can be improved. And they know that Scientology works.

Use what you read in these pages to help yourself and others and you will too.

CHURCH OF SCIENTOLOGY INTERNATIONAL

*M*an has long found ethics to be a confusing subject. In recent decades it has become more so. How does a person know if what he is doing is right or wrong? When he sees dishonest men hold power, criminals go free and traditional values cast aside, maybe he feels he should take the easy way out. "Others cheat on their taxes, why shouldn't I?" "Other kids shoplift, what's the harm?" But, regardless of anything else, a person has to live with himself. With many pressures pushing and pulling at a person, how can he be sure his choices will be best for himself, his family and every aspect of his life and his future?

L. Ron Hubbard achieved a remarkable breakthrough in the field of ethics which included not only simplification and codification of the subject, but development of a workable technology with applicability to our daily lives, one which brings about increased happiness, prosperity and survival.

These fundamentals, taken from Mr. Hubbard's body of work, do not present the entirety of ethics technology available in Scientology. However, they do provide an exact means for an individual to gradually raise his ethics level, increase his survival potential in any area of life and help others do the same. Thus ethics technology is the key tool you need to succeed in **all** aspects of existence.

THE BASICS
OF ETHICS

Throughout the ages, man has struggled with the subjects of right and wrong and ethics and justice.

The dictionary defines *ethics* as "the study of the general nature of morals and of the specific moral choices to be made by the individual in his relationship with others."

The same dictionary defines *justice* as "conformity to moral right, or to reason, truth or fact," or "the administration of law."

As you can see, these terms have become confused.

All philosophies from time immemorial have involved themselves with these subjects. And they never solved them.

That they have been solved in Scientology is a breakthrough of magnitude. The solution lay, first, in their *separation*. From there it could go forward to a workable technology for each.

Ethics consists simply of the actions an individual takes on himself. It is a personal thing. When one is ethical or "has his ethics in," it is by his own determinism and is done by himself.

Justice is the action taken on the individual by the group when he fails to take these actions himself.

History

These subjects are, actually, the basis of all philosophy. But in any study of the history of philosophy it is plain that they have puzzled philosophers for a long time.

The early Greek followers of Pythagoras (Greek philosopher of the sixth century B.C.) tried to apply their mathematical theories to the subject of human conduct and ethics. Some time later, Socrates (Greek philosopher and teacher, 470?–399 B.C.) tackled the subject. He demonstrated that all those who were claiming to show people how to live were unable to defend their views or even define the terms they were using. He argued that we must know what courage, and justice, law and government are before we can be brave or good citizens or just or good rulers. This was fine, but he then refused to provide definitions. He said that all sin was ignorance but did not take the necessary actions to rid man of his ignorance.

Socrates' pupil, Plato (Greek philosopher, 427?–347 B.C.) adhered (held closely) to his master's theories but insisted that these definitions could only be defined by pure reason. This meant that one had to isolate oneself from life in some ivory tower and figure it all out—not very useful to the man in the street.

Aristotle (Greek philosopher, 384–322 B.C.) also got involved with ethics. He explained unethical behavior by saying that man's rationality became overruled by his desire.

This chain continued down the ages. Philosopher after philosopher tried to resolve the subjects of ethics and justice.

Unfortunately, until now, there has been no workable solution, as evidenced by the declining ethical level of society.

So you see it is no small breakthrough that has been made in this subject in the last thirty years or so. We have defined the terms, which Socrates omitted to do, and we have a workable technology that anyone can use to help get himself out of the mud. The natural laws behind this subject have been found and made available for all to use.

Ethics

Ethics is so native to the individual that when it goes off the rails he will always seek to overcome his own lack of ethics.

He knows he has an ethics blind spot the moment he develops it. At that moment he starts trying to put ethics in on himself, and to the degree that he can envision long-term survival concepts, he may be successful, even though lacking the actual tech of ethics.

All too often, however, an individual becomes involved in an out-ethics situation; and if the individual has no tech with which to handle it analytically (rationally), his "handling" is to believe or pretend that something was done to him that prompted or justified his out-ethics action, and at that point he starts downhill. When that happens, nobody puts him down the chute harder, really, than he does himself.

And, once on the way down, without the basic technology of ethics, he has no way of climbing back up the chute—he just collapses, directly and deliberately. And even though he has a lot of complexities in his life, and he has other people doing him in, it all starts with his lack of knowledge of the technology of ethics.

This, basically, is one of the primary tools he uses to dig himself out.

Basic Nature of Man

No matter how criminal an individual is, he will be trying, one way or another, to put ethics in on himself.

The individual who lacks any ethics technology is unable to put in ethics on himself and restrain himself from contrasurvival (against survival) actions, so he caves himself in. And the individual is not going to come alive unless he gets hold of the basic tech of ethics and applies it to himself and others. He may find it a little unpalatable (distasteful) at first, but when you're dying of malaria you don't usually complain about the taste of the quinine: you may not like it, but you sure drink it.

Justice

When the individual fails to put in his own ethics, the group takes action against him and this is called justice.

Man cannot be trusted with justice. The truth is, man cannot really be trusted with "punishment." With it he does not really seek discipline; he wreaks injustice. He dramatizes his inability to get his own ethics in by trying to get others to get their ethics in: examine what laughingly passes for "justice" in our current society. Many governments are so touchy about their divine rightness in judicial matters that you hardly open your mouth before they burst into uncontrolled violence. Getting into police hands is a catastrophe in its own right in many places, even when one is merely the plaintiff (the one bringing the lawsuit), much less the accused. Thus, social disturbance is at maximum in such areas.

When the technology of ethics isn't known, justice becomes an end-all in itself. And that just degenerates into a sadism, an unnatural cruelty. Governments, because they don't understand ethics, have "ethics committees," but these are all worded in the framework of justice. They are even violating the derivation of the word *ethics*. They write justice over into ethics continuously with medical ethics committees, psychological ethics committees, congressional committees, etc. These are all on the basis of justice because they don't really know what ethics is. They call it ethics but they initiate justice actions and they punish people and make it harder for them to get their own ethics in.

Proper justice is expected and has definite use. When a state of discipline does not exist, the whole group caves in. It has been noted continually that the failure of a group began with a lack of or loss of discipline. Without it the group and its members die. But you must understand ethics *and* justice. The individual can be trusted with ethics, and when he is taught to put his own ethics in, justice no longer becomes the all-important subject that it is made out to be.

Breakthrough

The breakthrough in Scientology is that we *do* have the basic technology of ethics. For the first time man *can* learn how to put his own ethics in and climb back up the chute.

This is a brand-new discovery; before Scientology it had never before seen the light of day, anywhere. It marks a turning point in the history of philosophy. The individual can learn this technology, learn to apply it to his life and can then put his own ethics in, change conditions and start heading upwards toward survival under his own steam.

Learn to use this technology very well for your own sake, for the sake of those around you and for the sake of the future of this culture as a whole.

THE CONDITIONS: STATES OF OPERATION

A condition is a state of existence. Everything is in one condition or another. The ethics conditions identify these states and provide formulas—exact steps which one can use to move from one condition to another higher and more survival condition.

Be it an organization or its parts or an individual, *everything* passes through various states of existence. These, if not handled properly, bring about shrinkage and misery and worry and death.

If handled properly they bring about stability, expansion, influence and well-being.

The formulas for these are the monitoring formulas for livingness (the state of living).

The conditions, ranged from highest to lowest, are:

Power

Power Change

Affluence

Normal Operation

Emergency

Danger

Non-Existence

Liability

Doubt

Enemy

Treason

Confusion

The first thing to know about them is that each step in a formula is in exact sequence and must be done in *that* sequence. It is totally fatal to reverse the order of sequence of two or more actions. If the sequence is disordered the final result is a smaller organization or less influential person.

A key datum is that if the formulas are not known or correctly applied, an organism emerges from each crisis smaller.

A person can exist in different conditions. Ethics is the means by which he can raise himself to a higher condition and improve his survival.

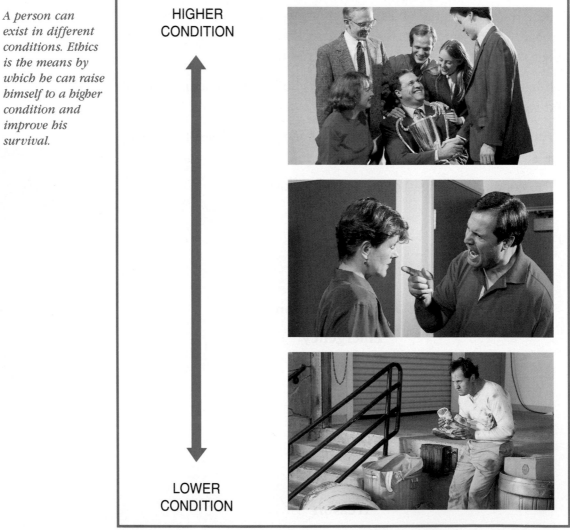

HIGHER
CONDITION

LOWER
CONDITION

THE MEASUREMENT OF SURVIVAL: STATISTICS

The next thing to know about applying the correct formula to a condition is that one knows this only by closely and continually inspecting statistics. By statistics is meant numbers of things, measurement of volume, all relative to time. A statistic not compared to the same type of statistic earlier will not predict any future statistic. A single statistic is meaningless. Statistics are always worse than, the same as or better than they were at an earlier time. Graphing statistics and the reading of graphs is a vital necessity, then, in monitoring an organization, department or person and applying conditions formulas to it.

This is much easier than it appears. If you made $20,000 last year and only $15,000 this year, you obviously are slipping; if you made $30,000 this year you are pretty stable; if you made $50,000 this year you are affluent—all compared to the $20,000 you made last year. What are the codes of conduct you should use to stay healthy under these *conditions?* These are the conditions formulas.

The third thing to know is that one can wreck an organization or department or person by applying the wrong condition formula. The universe is made that way. The right condition must be applied.

READING STATISTICS

The reason one reads a graph is so one can see what is happening with a statistic. Is it improving? Is it getting worse? The value of being able to do this is so one can determine which of the conditions formulas one needs to apply to either keep a statistic rising if it is already going up or halt its slide and get it going up if it is falling.

This applies to an individual, a group or a whole organization. It applies to *any* production activity.

In a local organization area one reads the division stats for the *week*. A department reads its stats by the *day*. A section does it by the *hour*. You can also read all main statistics by the day; successful organizations and people do.

Statistic *trends*—meaning the tendency of statistics to average out up, level or down over several *weeks*—are used in more remote areas from the organization to indicate successful leadership or broad organizational situations. Trends are used locally to estimate expansion or warn of contraction.

To determine a stat trend one looks at several weeks' worth of statistics. For example, a regional manager would use three weeks' worth of statistics to manage with whereas an executive in charge of a whole continent would use a period of six weeks' statistics with which to manage.

In short, when you are close up to a statistic (close to where the actual product is being produced) you can do something about it and when you are far away, the day's worth of stats has already changed before any order could arrive.

In weekly condition assignments one only considers two things: that exact week and the slant of that one line.

The following are examples of statistics kept on a weekly basis and what the condition assignments would be.

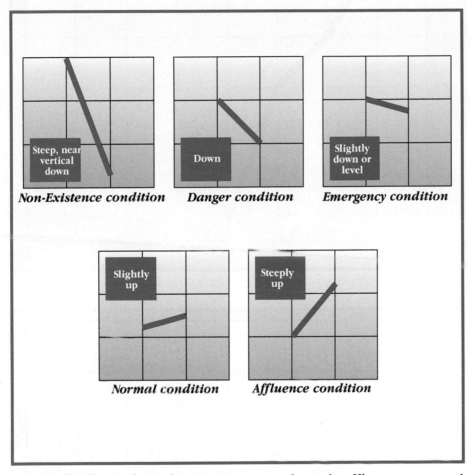

Non-Existence condition   **Danger condition**   **Emergency condition**

Normal condition   **Affluence condition**

Note that these slants for Non-Existence through Affluence are used to determine the stat condition *for the week*.

Statistic *trends* are read over a three- or six-week period or longer.

The following examples show various statistic trends and the conditions that would be assigned.

A Non-Existence *trend* would look like this (plotted by weeks):

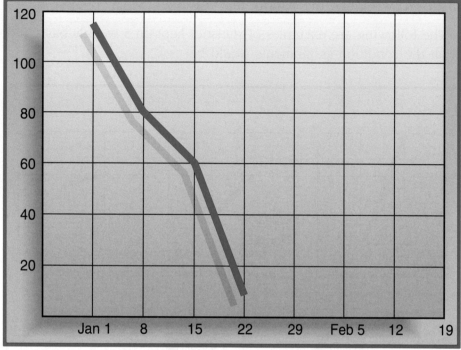

A stat in a completely nonviable range would also be a Non-Existence *trend*.

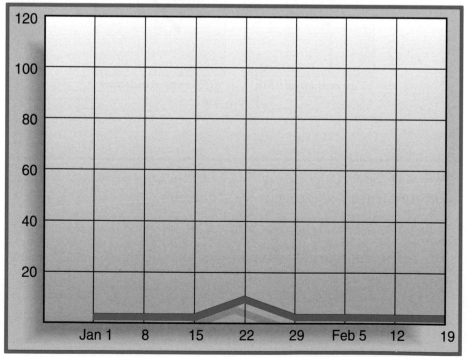

This would be a Danger *trend*:

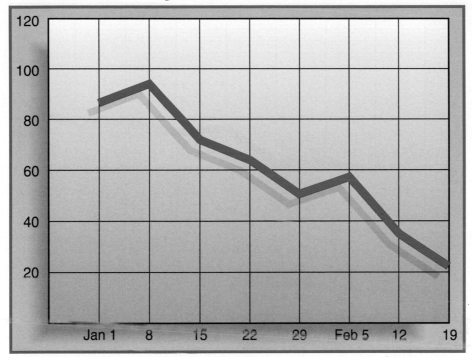

This would be an Emergency *trend*:

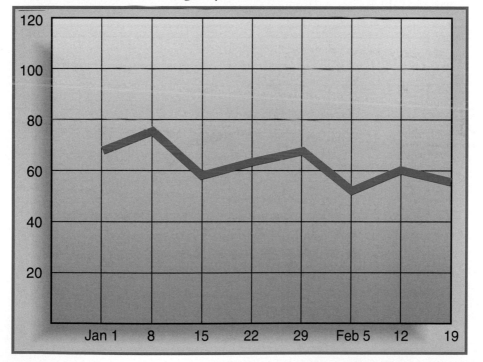

This would be a Normal *trend:*

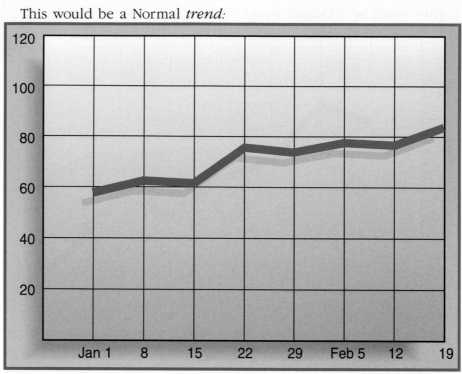

Any slight rise above level is Normal.

This would be an Affluence *trend:*

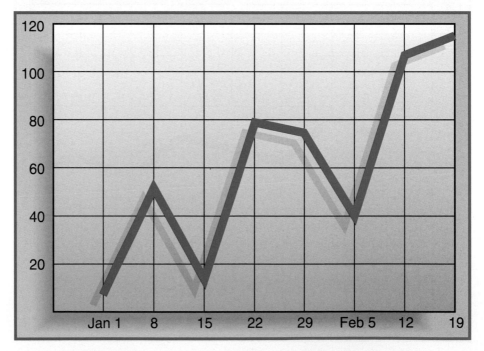

Power is a *trend,* it is not judged on a one-week basis only nor by a single line on a graph. Power is a Normal trend maintained in a high, high range; thus a Power condition must be determined by more than one week's worth of stats.

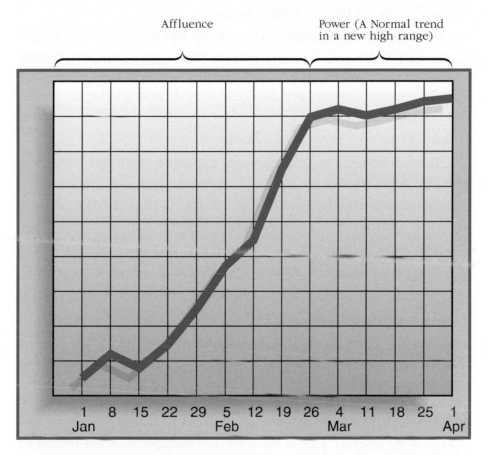

Affluence

Power (A Normal trend in a new high range)

1 8 15 22 29 5 12 19 26 4 11 18 25 1
Jan   Feb   Mar   Apr

If you accurately manage by statistics and apply the condition formula for the area based on the statistic and do this every week, the organization will start to occupy more space, need more people, need more equipment. Actually, the area control of the organization or activity increases, and stability and viability increase.

If stat declines for the week are brushed off (ignored), the organization or activity will shrink, become less stable, will demand more work by fewer and will be a burden.

When you manage by the stat, you don't go wrong.

Properly Scaling Statistic Graphs

A statistic graph is not informative if its vertical scale results in graph line changes that are too small. It is not possible to draw the graph at all if the line changes are too large.

If the ups and downs are not plainly visible on a graph, then those interpreting the graph make errors. What is shown as a flat-looking line really should be a mountain range.

By *scale* is meant the number of anything per vertical inch of graph.

The scale is different for every statistic. For example, one would have a different scale for the graph of the product produced by a company, such as repaired automobiles, than one would have for the income of that company.

The way to do a scale is as follows:

1. Determine the lowest amount one expects a particular statistic to go—this is not always zero.

2. Determine the highest amount one can believe the statistic will go in the next three months. (Graphed weekly.)

3. Subtract (1) from (2).

4. Proportion (adjust in relation to) the vertical divisions as per (3).

Your scale will then be quite real and show up its rises and falls.

Here is an *incorrect* example.

We take a factory that produces 5,000 bicycles per week. We proportion the vertical marks of the graph paper, of which there are 100, so each one represents 1,000 bicycles. This when graphed will show a low line, quite flat, no matter what the organization's production is doing and so draws no attention from executives when it rises and dives.

This is the *correct* way to do it for the number of units produced of a company averaging 5,000 bicycles produced per week.

1. Looking over the old graphs of the past six months we find it never went under 2,400 bicycles produced. So we take 2,000 as the lowest point of the graph paper.

2. We estimate this organization should get up to 12,000 in the next three months, so we take this as the top of the graph paper.

3. We subtract 2,000 from 12,000 and we have 10,000.

4. We take the 100 blocks of vertical and make each one 100 bicycles produced, starting with 2,000 as the lowest mark.

Now we plot product as 100 bicycles per graph division.

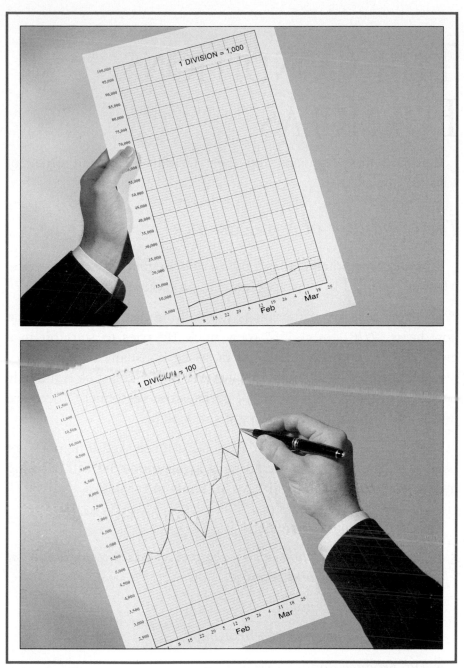

This will look right, show falls and rises very clearly and so will be of use to executives in interpretation.

Try to use easily computed units like 5, 10, 25, 50, 100, and show the scale itself on the graph (1 division = 100).

Correct scaling is the essence of good graphing. And with good graphing one can easily and accurately read statistics to determine the correct condition formula to apply.

THE CONDITIONS FORMULAS

Here are the conditions and their formulas given in order of advance upward:

The Condition of Non-Existence

Every new appointee to a post or job begins in Non-Existence, whether obtained by new appointment, promotion or demotion.

The new person on the job is normally under the delusion that now he is "*THE* _____" (new title). He tries to start off in a much higher condition than he is in, as he is usually very aware of his new status or even a former status. But in actual fact *he* is the only one aware of it. All others except perhaps the Personnel Officer are utterly unaware of him as having his new status.

Therefore he begins in a state of Non-Existence. And if he does not begin with the Non-Existence Formula as his guide, he will be using the wrong condition and will have all kinds of trouble.

<u>The Non-Existence Formula is</u>:

1. *Find a communication line—a channel on which communication can be sent out and received.*

2. *Make yourself known.*

3. *Discover what is needed or wanted.*

4. *Do, produce and/or present it.*

A new appointee taking over a going concern often thinks he had better make himself known by changing everything, whereas he (a) is not well enough known to do so and (b) hasn't any idea of what is needed or wanted yet. And so he makes havoc.

Sometimes he assumes he knows what is needed or wanted when it is only a fixed idea with him and is only his idea and not true at all and so he fails at his job.

Sometimes he doesn't bother to find out what is really needed or wanted and simply assumes it or thinks he knows when he doesn't. He soon becomes "unsuccessful."

Now and then a new appointee is so "status happy" or so insecure or so shy that even when his boss or his staff comes to him and tells him what is needed or wanted he can't or doesn't even acknowledge and really does go into Non-Existence for keeps.

Sometimes he finds that what he is *told* is needed or wanted needs reappraisal or further investigation. So it is always safest for him to make his own survey of it and operate on it when he gets his own firm reality on what is needed or wanted.

If the formula is applied intelligently, the person can expect to get into a zone of bypass where people are still doing his job to fill the hole his predecessor may have left. This is a Danger condition—but it is the next one higher than Non-Existence on the scale. If he defends his job and does his job and applies the Danger Formula, he will come through it.

He can then expect to find himself in an Emergency condition. In this he must follow the Emergency Formula with his post and he will come through *it.*

He can now expect to be in Normal Operation, and if he follows the formula of that, he will come to Affluence. And if he follows *that* formula, he will arrive at Power. And if he applies the Power Formula, he will stay there.

So it is a long way from Power that one starts his new appointment, and if he doesn't go *up* the scale from where he really is at the start, he will of course fail.

This applies to groups, to organizations, to countries as well as individuals.

It also applies when a person fails at his job. He has to start again at Non-Existence and he will build up the same way condition by condition.

Most failures on post are occasioned by failures to follow the conditions and recognize them and apply the formula of the condition one is in when one is in it and cease to apply it when one is out of it and in another.

This is the secret of holding a post and being successful on a job or in life.

Non-Existence Formula Expanded

Many people misapply the Non-Existence Formula and then wonder why they seem to continue to have trouble.

Executives sometimes wonder why certain staff personnel never seem to be able to do anything right and out of exasperation wind up handling the whole area themselves.

The answer is a misapplication of and not really doing the Non-Existence Formula on their job.

Experience has shown that even experienced executives and staff members have not in fact ever come out of Non-Existence. And where the organization runs at all, it is carried on the back of one or two key seniors.

The phrase "find a communication line" is shortened down by too many to locating somebody's in-basket and dropping a "needed and wanted" request in it. This is not really finding a communication line.

To handle *any* post you have to have *information* and furnish *information*. Where this is not done, the person finds himself doing projects that get rejected, projects that have to be redone, restraints put on his actions and finds himself sinking down the conditions. He gets in bad with his seniors *because he doesn't acquire and doesn't furnish* the vital information of *what is going on*.

It is the duty of any staff member, new on post or not, *to round up the communication lines that relate to his post, find out who needs vital information from him and get those lines in, in, in* as a continuing action.

When a person fails to do just that, he never comes out of Non-Existence. He isn't even up to Danger because nobody knows they are even bypassing him. In other words, when a staff member does not do that, in the eyes of the organization, he is simply a *zero*.

Orders being issued by him usually wind up *cancelled* when discovered by some senior because they are not real. Joe was already handling it. Bill's schedule was thrown out by it. Treasury yells, "How come this wasted expense?"

Pretty soon, when staff hears it's so-and-so's order they just ignore it.

The bright hopes of such a person usually wind up as hopes he will be able to get transferred, the sooner the better. Everybody is against him.

But what really happened?

He never applied the Non-Existence Formula for real and so he stayed in Non-Existence. His actions do not coordinate because he *does not have the lines to give or receive information*.

It is really and factually not up to anyone else to round up his communication lines for him any more than it is up to others to do his breathing for him. The inhale and exhale of an organization or any activity is the take and give of *vital information and particles* (objects or communications).

Anyone who finds himself in apparent Non-Existence or worse should rush around and find the communication lines that apply to his activity and post and insist that he be put on those lines.

Such a person, staff member or executive has to write down what information he has to have to handle his post and what information others have to have from him to do their jobs.

And then arrange communication lines so that he is an info addressee from secretaries on those lines.

Senior executives such as division heads or heads of an organization do have a responsibility for briefing staff. But they are usually also faced with security problems as well as a wish to look good. And their data is general for the whole division or organization. It does include specifics like "Mrs. Zikes is arriving at 1400 hours" or "the telephone company rep says the bill must be paid by 1200 hours today or we got no phones."

Havoc and overwork for executives occur where the bulk of the staff have omitted to get themselves on important communication lines and keep those lines flowing. Do not send to find why the statistics are down if 90 percent of your staff is in Non-Existence or worse! Simply because they never really found any communication lines.

Therefore the Expanded Non-Existence Formula is:

1. *Find and get yourself on every communication line you will need in order to give and obtain information relating to your duties and materiel.*

2. *Make yourself known, along with your post title and duties, to every person you will need for the obtaining of information and the giving of data.*

3. *Discover from your seniors and fellow staff members and any public your duties may require you to contact, what is needed and wanted from each.*

4. *Do, produce and present what each needs and wants that is in conformation with (in agreement with) policy.*

5. *Maintain your communication lines that you have and expand them to obtain other information you now find you need on a routine basis.*

6. *Maintain your origination lines to inform others what you are doing exactly, but only those who actually need the information.*

7. *Streamline what you are doing, producing and presenting so that it is more closely what is really needed and wanted.*

8. *With full information being given and received concerning your products, do, produce and present a greatly improved product routinely on your post.*

If you do this—and write your information concisely so it is quick to grasp and get your data in a form that doesn't jam your own communication lines—you will start on up the conditions for actual and in due course arrive in Power.

The Condition of Danger

As a person or activity moves up the scale from Non-Existence, the condition of Danger is reached.

A Danger condition also exists where statistics show continuing Emergency or a steep, steep fall.

Three formulas exist for handling a Danger condition: (a) the Senior Danger Formula, for a superior at work, or the head of a family or group who finds that a Danger condition exists in an area under his responsibility; (b) the Junior Danger Formula, which is assigned by a senior or executive to a junior whose job he is forced to do; and (c) the Individual Danger Formula, for the individual who finds himself in Danger.

Senior Danger Formula

The *Senior* Danger Formula is the formula an executive himself applies when he assigns a junior or area under his control a condition of Danger. It is assigned under the following circumstances:

A. When a statistic plunges downward very steeply

B. When an executive suddenly finds himself or herself doing the job of the head of the activity because it is in trouble

C. When an Emergency condition (the next condition upward in the sequence) has continued too long

<u>The formula for the condition of Senior Danger is:</u>

1. *Bypass (ignore the junior normally in charge of the activity and handle it personally).*

2. *Handle the situation and any danger in it.*

3. *Assign the area where it had to be handled a Danger condition.*

4. *Assign each individual connected with the Danger condition an Individual Danger condition and enforce and ensure that they follow the formula completely, and if they do not do so, do a full ethics investigation and take all actions indicated.*

5. *Reorganize the activity so that the situation does not repeat.*

6. *Recommend any firm policy that will hereafter detect and/or prevent the condition from recurring.*

To *bypass* someone means to "jump the proper terminal (person or post) in a chain of command."

If you declare a Danger condition, you must do the work necessary to handle the situation that is dangerous.

This is also true in reverse, meaning that if you start doing the work of another on a bypass you will of course unwittingly bring about a Danger condition. Why? Because you are making nothing of the people who should be doing the work.

If you habitually do the work of others on a bypass, you will of course inherit all the work. This is the answer to the overworked executive. He or she bypasses. It's as simple as that. If an executive habitually bypasses, he or she will then become overworked.

Also the condition of Non-Existence will occur.

So the more an executive bypasses, the harder he works. The harder he works on a bypass, the more the section he is working on will disappear.

So purposely or unwittingly working on a bypass, the result is always the same—a Danger condition.

If you *have* to do the work on a bypass, you *must* get the condition declared and follow the formula.

If you declare the condition, you must also do the work.

You must get the work being competently done by new appointment or transfer or training of personnel. The condition is over when that portion of the company or organization has visibly, statistically recovered.

So there are great responsibilities in declaring a Danger condition. These are outweighed in burdensomeness by the fact that if you *don't* declare one on functions handled by those under you which go bad, it will very soon catch up with you yourself, willy-nilly, and declared or not, *you* will go into a Danger condition personally.

There's the frying pan—there's the fire. The cheerful note about it is that if the formula is applied, you have a good chance of not only rising again but also of being bigger and better than ever.

And that's the first time *that* ever happened to an executive who started down the long slide. There's hope!

Junior Danger Formula

This formula is called the "Junior" Danger Formula because it is assigned by an employer (or "senior") to his employee (or "junior") when the senior suddenly finds himself or herself forced into doing the junior's job and/or the statistics of the junior are in Danger. In other words, he assigns the condition because an area below him that is under his control is in Danger. (That is not the only time the Junior Danger Formula would be done. A person would do the Junior Danger Formula if his own personal statistic were in a condition of Danger, regardless of any senior's intervention and without waiting for anyone to assign it to him.)

Where a Danger condition is assigned to a junior, request that he or she or the entire activity write up his or her overts and withholds and any known out-ethics situation and turn them in at a certain stated time on a basis that the penalty for them will be lessened but if discovered later after the deadline it will be doubled.

Overts are intentionally committed harmful acts done in an effort to resolve a problem. They are those things which you do which you aren't willing to have happen to you.

Withholds are unspoken, unannounced transgressions against a moral code by which the person was bound. Things the person did that he or she is not talking about. A withhold is always the manifestation which comes after an overt. Any withhold comes after an overt.

This write-up done, require that the junior and the staff that had to be bypassed and whose work had to be done for them or continually corrected, each one write up and fully execute the Individual Danger Formula for himself personally and turn it in.

Individual Danger Formula

<u>The Individual Danger Formula is</u>:

1. *Bypass habits or normal routines.*

2. *Handle the situation and any danger in it.*

3. *Assign self a Danger condition.*

4. *Get in your own <u>personal ethics</u> by finding what you are doing that is out-ethics and use self-discipline to correct it and get honest and straight.*

5. *Reorganize your life so that the dangerous situation is not continually happening to you.*

6. *Formulate and adopt firm policy that will hereafter detect and prevent the same situation from continuing to occur.*

Here is an example of how the Individual Danger Formula could be applied.

The first step is (1) Bypass habits and normal routines. In other words, "bypass doing all this stuff you've been doing!"

Let us say a fellow was accepting money from his uncle, saying that he was buying a house with it when he wasn't. He was spending the money on a blonde, staying up late, not doing his job at work and because of this his own personal income was in a steep, steep fall. Now he's in continuous danger. His uncle might find out about it at any moment.

And because the fellow expects to inherit his uncle's fortune some day, he's in a sort of panic.

To apply the Danger condition, he bypasses the habits or normal routines that might be causing the situation. In other words, he's got to bypass doing all that stuff he's been doing: He had better quit accepting the money from his uncle!

The next step is (2) Handle the situation and any danger in it.

Now, it would be very dangerous to write "Dear Uncle George: For the last year and a half, all the money you've been sending me to buy a house with, I have been spending on a blonde named Floozie." He would have to figure out how to handle that so that there wasn't any danger in it. And it might take quite a bit of thinking.

If he just jumped up and said to his uncle, "Well, I've been lying to you, Uncle George. I've been wasting all of your dough," the possibility is that it would come as such a shock to Uncle George that he would disinherit him, shoot him and so forth. Then the fellow would really be in danger. So he has to figure out how to handle it. It might be as simple as "Dear Uncle George: I have become a more honest man. Now, there are many dishonest things which I have done in my life and one of them is this. Now, you will probably shoot me for having done this, but actually I am using this money and I am using some of it to live on, and that is not fair to you."

The next step, (3), Assign self a Danger condition, is only there because people forget to assign it. It has to be assigned.

The next step is (4) Get in your own personal ethics by finding what you are doing that is out-ethics and use self-discipline to correct it and get honest and straight.

There might be some other "Uncle Georges." Though you have to handle Uncle George and the blonde named Floozie, there may be more situations that haven't been mentioned, and this must be watched for. If missed, such unhandled situations can effectively block a person's handling.

With these steps done, a person is now able to face the world and get back into communication. The formula is quite interesting from that point of view.

The next step is (5) Reorganize your life so that the dangerous situation is not continually happening to you.

Well, that's easy in this hypothetical case above. He simply stops doing whatever it was that caused this situation. Instead of being up all night every night, he actually gets some sleep and does his job and amounts to something. He makes more money this way and can save up enough money to buy his own house. That's a reorganization of his life.

And then, (6) Formulate and adopt firm policy that will hereafter detect and prevent the same situation from continuing to occur.

In other words, "I'm not going to tell lies so I can get money," or something like that, is all a guy would have to decide. It's actually asking the person at this point to reform. It's like a New Year's resolution. (People who don't keep such resolutions don't because they didn't get in the first five steps!)

And that completes the Individual Danger Formula.

The Condition of Emergency

It is an empirical (observed and proven by observation) fact that nothing remains exactly the same forever. This condition is foreign to this universe. Things grow or they lessen. They cannot apparently maintain the same equilibrium (balance) or stability.

Thus things either expand or they contract. They do not remain level in this universe. Further, when something seeks to remain level and unchanged, it contracts.

Thus we have three actions and only three. First is expansion, second is the effort to remain level or unchanged and third is contraction or lessening.

As nothing in this universe can remain exactly the same, then the

An unchanging or slightly worsening condition requires application of the Emergency Formula.

30

second action (level) above will become the third action (lessen) if undisturbed or not acted on by an outside force. Thus actions two and three above (level and lessen) are similar in potential and both will lessen.

This leaves expansion as the only positive action which tends to guarantee survival.

To survive, then, one must expand as the only safe condition of operation.

If one remains level, one tends to contract. If one contracts, one's chances of survival diminish.

Therefore, there is only one chance left and that, for an organization or an individual, is expansion.

In order to expand in such a situation, one needs to apply the formula for a condition of Emergency.

One is apt to become more familiar with Emergency than with the other formulas in the early stages of life or organization. There is a tendency to become conditioned to it and continue to use it as a prevention. However, if one continues to apply Emergency when one is in Normal Operation things can disrupt and shrink. So a condition of Emergency must be ended when it is actually over. Otherwise it will become the wrong formula to be applying.

One applies the condition of Emergency when:

1. Statistics of an organization, department or portion of an organization or a person are seen to be *declining.* The larger the organism, the greater the time span that must be applied.

2. Unchanging statistics of an organization or a portion of an organization or a person. This must be judged on overall statistics on a longer line basis (statistical trend). No real change down or up means a condition of Emergency.

People in this society are commonly accustomed to being in an Emergency condition, either by decline or excessive stability of the graph. Life therefore looks pretty hopeless and frantic. The American civilization is founded on a continuous state of personal or business emergency and never drops it when it is ended so passes unknowingly into the condition of Normal Operation, still applying the remedies for

Emergency and collapses back into Emergency by reason of applying a wrong (and misunderstood) formula.

One can't stand still in this universe. If one does, the result is shrinkage of influence, size and eventual decline and collapse.

The formula for the condition of Emergency is:

1. *Promote. That applies to an organization. To an individual you had better say produce.*

That's the first action regardless of any other action. Regardless of anything else, that is the first thing you have to put attention on. The first broad, big action which you take is promote. Exactly what is promotion? It is making things known; it is getting things out; it is getting oneself known, getting one's products out.

2. *Change your operating basis.*

If for instance you went into a condition of Emergency and then you didn't change after you had promoted, you didn't make any changes in your operation, well, you just head for another condition of Emergency.

So that has to be part of it; you had better change your operating basis; you had better do something to change the operating basis, because that operating basis led you into an emergency so you sure better change it.

3. *Economize.*

4. *Prepare to deliver.*

5. *Stiffen discipline.*

To an individual this could simply mean "not to go down to the pub every Friday night." Or, "Let's stiffen up the discipline, let's stay home and work and burn some midnight oil." "Let's stay home and do some homework." "Let's be a little more regular on the job, work a little harder." "Let's not goof quite so much and make so many mistakes."

If in an organization, the individuals involved have been assigned a condition of Emergency and are still found to be goofing, what do you do? The statistic is going down and continues to go down. There is only one thing left to do and that is discipline, because if discipline is not put in, life itself is going to discipline the individual.

The Condition of Normal Operation

The condition of Normal Operation does not mean "stability," as there is no such thing as a no-increase, no-decrease state.

To prevent a deterioration you must have an increase. That increase doesn't have to be spectacular but it has to be something. **There is an exact way this condition is handled**:

1. *The way you maintain an increase is when you are in a state of Normal Operation you don't change anything.*

2. *Ethics are very mild, the justice factor is quite mild, there are no savage actions taken particularly.*

3. *When a statistic betters then look it over carefully and find out what bettered it, and then do that without abandoning what you were doing before.*

4. *Every time a statistic worsens slightly, quickly find out why and remedy it.*

In a condition of Normal Operation there are no rough or desperate actions taken. If one of your employees is sitting around in an old shirt, let him sit around in an old shirt. Maybe that is part of the increase—you don't know for sure.

What you do in a Normal Operation condition is very carefully examine every slightest rise in a statistic. Every time a statistic betters, look it over carefully and find out what bettered it and then do that. Those are the only changes you make.

And every time a statistic worsens slightly, quickly find out why and remedy it. When you find a statistic worsening you will find out inevitably that some change has been made, and you had better get that change out of the way in a hurry.

You just jockey those two factors: the statistic bettering, the statistic worsening.

Regula
expans
increa:
a cond
Norma
exists.

*When taking
over a successful
position, a
condition of
Power Change
exists.*

The Condition of Power Change

Correctly applying the condition of Power Change makes it possible for a person to successfully take over a job his predecessor left behind.

There are only two circumstances which require replacement, the very successful one or the very unsuccessful one.

What a song it is to inherit a successful pair of boots; there is nothing to it; just step in the boots and don't bother to walk. If it was in a normal state of operation, which it normally would have been in for anybody to have been promoted out of it, you just don't change anything.

If anybody wants something signed that your predecessor would not have signed, don't sign it. The thing to do is to be alert and learn the ropes of the new job and, depending on how big the organization is, after a certain time, inspect how it is running and run it as a Normal condition.

Go through the exact same routine every day that your predecessor went through. Sign nothing that he wouldn't sign, don't change a single order. Look through the papers that had been issued at that period of time when he was on post, the ones that are still in existence, and get busy enforcing those. The operation will continue to increase.

If you walk into the boots of somebody who has left the area in disgrace, you had better apply the Emergency Formula to it, starting with the promote step.

Power Change Violation Repair Formula

Many people, unfortunately, do not correctly follow the Power Change Formula. The old adage (saying) of a "new broom sweeps clean" applied to an area that was in Power can send it into a rapid tailspin.

A Danger condition can be brought about by a violation of the Power Change condition.

<u>The formula for repairing a violation of the Power Change Formula is</u>:

1. *Observe, question and draw up a list of what was previously successful in your area or zone of control.*

2. *Observe and draw up a list of all those things that were unsuccessful in your area in the past.*

3. *Get the successful actions IN.*

4. *Throw the unsuccessful actions out.*

5. *Knock off frantically trying to cope with the demands of the job or defend your position.*

6. *Sensibly get back in a working structure.*

The Condition of Power

A Power condition is not simply a high Affluence condition.

Power is a Normal condition in a stellar range so high that it is total abundance, no doubt about it.

It is a statistic that has gone up into a whole new, steeply high range and maintained that range and now, in that new high range, is on a Normal trend.

It is not a line that has gone straight up on the graph. It is a stable increase in an entirely new range.

Operating in this new range you may get a slight dip in that statistic now and then. But it is still Power.

There is another datum that is of importance if one is to correctly recognize and understand this condition:

Why do we call it Power?

Because there is such an abundance of production there that momentary halts or dips can't pull it down or imperil its survival.

And *that* is *Power.*

<u>Here is the Power Formula</u>.

1. *The first law of a condition of Power is don't disconnect. You cannot deny your connections. What you have to do is take ownership and responsibility for your connections.*

2. *The first thing you have to do is make a record of all of the connections and communication channels of the job or area that is in Power. That is the only way you will ever be able to move on as in a promotion. Therefore, in a condition of Power the first thing you have to do is write up your whole job. This is the thing which makes it possible for the next person to take over your position and assume the state of Power Change.*

   If you are in Power but don't write up your whole job, you are going to be stuck with a piece of that job forever, and a year or so later somebody will still be coming to you asking you about that job which you held.

3. *Your responsibility is to write up a detailed description of the job, its functions and duties in all its aspects and get it into the hands of the person who is going to assume the job.*

4. *Do all you can to make the job occupiable.*

COMPLETING CONDITIONS FORMULAS

The ethics conditions formulas flow in sequence, one to the next, with the first step of one formula directly following the final step of the previous formula.

What do you do if your statistic indicates you've moved up a condition before you even have a chance to finish a formula? Do you just drop that formula and start on the next one? The answer is *no*. One completes the formula he has begun.

Here's an example. The head of an organization, in looking over his statistics, sees that they are in Emergency. He immediately sees to it that the *promote* step of the Emergency Formula is begun. Once that is well in hand he begins to *change his operating basis*. He gets on-the-job training actions being done on some of his key staff and hires some specialists.

But before he has a chance to do each of the remaining steps of the Emergency Formula, the statistics move up into Normal Operation.

What does he do? Well, he is now in a condition of Normal by statistics. But the Normal Formula would also cause him to complete the Emergency Formula, because in the Normal Formula you drop out what is unsuccessful and you push what was successful; what was successful here was the Emergency Formula. Thus, this executive can get continued improvement by *completing* the

Emergency Formula, as the actions on the Emergency Formula are what got him to Normal so quickly. So he would push them until they were completed fully. This doesn't mean he is still in an Emergency condition—the statistics are now rising and the condition *is* Normal. It is a bit of an unusual situation.

That one's statistics rise before completing a formula doesn't mean he cannot go into the higher condition his statistics now indicate. However, if undone steps of an earlier formula are not completed, one could soon find his statistics down again. So, as in the above example, one has to complete the earlier formula, then complete the next formula and continue on as his statistics dictate.

You will not always get a statistic rise before you have a chance to fully complete a formula. But one had better make sure every step of each condition formula is fully *done*.

Completing a formula is very vital. One doesn't just name a formula. He gets it *completed*.

We have now covered each of the conditions from Non-Existence to Power.

These are exactly delineated states. Their formulas, followed, are tools by which anyone can improve any aspect of his life and build for himself a life of success and fulfillment.

Conditions Below Non-Existence

There also exist operating states below Non-Existence.

The question might arise, "How could there be a condition *below* Non-Existence?" This occurs where a person or group is no longer just a zero (nonexistent) but has become actively detrimental to survival and progress. The degrees of destructiveness are reflected in the conditions below Non-Existence. There are five of these conditions, the first of which is Liability.

The Condition of Liability

In the condition of Liability, the individual has ceased to be simply nonexistent as a team member and has taken on the color of an enemy.

It is assigned where careless or malicious and knowing damage is caused to projects, organizations or activities. It is adjudicated that it is malicious and knowing because orders have been published against it or because it is contrary to the intentions and actions of the remainder of the team or the purpose of the project or organization.

It is a *liability* to have such a person unwatched as the person may do or continue to do things to stop or impede the forward progress of the project or organization and such a person cannot be trusted. No discipline or the assignment of conditions above it has been of any avail. The person has just kept on messing it up.

The condition is usually assigned when several Dangers and Non-Existences have been assigned or when a long unchanged pattern of conduct has been detected.

When one drops into a state where he is detrimental to the group he is supposed to serve, a condition of Liability exists.

The condition is assigned for the benefit of others so they won't get tripped up trusting the person in any way.

The formula of Liability is:

1. *Decide who are one's friends.*

2. *Deliver an effective blow to the enemies of the group one has been pretending to be part of despite personal danger.*

3. *Make up the damage one has done by personal contribution far beyond the ordinary demands of a group member.*

4. *Apply for re-entry to the group by asking the permission of each member of it to rejoin and rejoining only by majority permission, and if refused, repeating (2) and (3) and (4) until one is allowed to be a group member again.*

The Condition of Doubt

When one cannot make up one's mind as to an individual, a group, organization or project, a condition of Doubt exists.

If one cannot come to a decision about a situation, a condition of Doubt exists.

The formula is:

1. *Inform oneself honestly of the actual intentions and activities of that group, project or organization, brushing aside all bias and rumor.*

2. *Examine the statistics of the individual, group, project or organization.*

3. *Decide on the basis of "the greatest good for the greatest number of people and areas of life" whether or not it should be attacked, harmed or suppressed or helped.*

4. *Evaluate oneself or one's own group, project or organization as to intentions and objectives.*

5. *Evaluate one's own or one's group, project or organization's statistics.*

6. *Join or remain in or befriend the one which progresses toward the greatest good for the greatest number and announce the fact publicly to both sides.*

7. *Do everything possible to improve the actions and statistics of the person, group, project or organization one has remained in or joined.*

8. *Suffer on up through the conditions in the new group if one has changed sides or the conditions of the group one has remained in if wavering from it has lowered one's status.*

The Condition of Enemy

When a person is an avowed and knowing enemy of an individual, a group, project or an organization, a condition of Enemy exists.

Destructive actions indicate a condition of Enemy.

<u>The formula for the condition of Enemy is just one step.</u>

Find out who you really are.

The Condition of Treason

Treason is defined as betrayal after trust.

It will be found, gruesomely enough, that a person who accepts a job or position and then doesn't function as it, will inevitably upset or destroy some portion of an organization.

Someone who betrays another after they trusted him is in a condition of Treason.

By not knowing that he is the _____ (job title), he is committing treason in fact.

The results of this can be found in history. A failure to be what one has the job or position name of will result in a betrayal of the functions and purposes of a group.

Almost all organizational upsets stem from this one fact:

A person in a group who, having accepted a job, does not know *that* he is a certain assigned or designated beingness is in *treason* against the group.

The formula for the condition of Treason is:

*Find out **that** you are.*

The Condition of Confusion

There is a condition below Treason.

It is a condition of Confusion.

In a condition of Confusion the being or area will be in a state of random motion. There will be no real production, only disorder or confusion.

In order to get out of Confusion one has to find out where he is.

It will be seen that the progress upward would be, in Confusion, find out where you are; in Treason, find out that you are; and for Enemy, find out who you are.

Random, useless activity with no actual production indicates a condition of Confusion.

The formula for Confusion is:

Find out where you are.

The additional formula for the condition of Confusion is:

1. *Locational Processing on the area in which one is.*

Locational Processing is a Scientology technique done to orient and put a person in communication with his environment. This is done by pointing out certain objects and telling the person to "Look at that _____ (object)" and acknowledging the person when he has done so. The objects could include such things as a tree, a building, a street, etc. This is done until the person is happier and has some kind of realization.

2. *Comparing where one is to other areas where one was.*

3. *Repeat step 1.*

Conditions Application

A vital thing to realize is that the formulas of conditions exist. They are part and parcel of any activity in this universe and now that they are known they must be complied with. This takes about 90 percent of chance out of all the activities of life and enables one to almost invariably raise himself into higher and higher levels of survival. The variables are only how well one estimates the situation and how energetic one is in applying the formulas.

The proper application of the proper formula works. It works no matter how stupidly it is applied only so long as the *right* formula is applied and the exact sequence of steps is taken. Brilliance only shows up in the *speed* of recovery or expansion. Very brilliant applications show up in overnight, sound expansions. Dull applications, given only that they are correct, show up in slower expansions. In other words, nobody has to be a screaming genius to apply them or dream up the necessary ideas in them. One only has to estimate the condition accurately and *act* energetically in applying its steps in exact order. The brighter the ideas, the faster the expansion, that's all. The expansion or gain is itself inevitable. However, if the dullness includes adding needless steps, then one may fail, and if one is so stupid that a wrong estimate is made of conditions and a wrong formula is applied and applied with its steps in wrong sequence, then one jolly well deserves to fail!

Another thing to know is that these conditions apply to a universe, a civilization, an organization, a portion of an organization or a person alike.

The final thing to know is that knowing the formulas carries the responsibility of using them. Otherwise one could be accused of willful suicide! For these *are* the formulas. And they do work like magic.

If these formulas are not known or used, expansion is totally a matter of chance or fate, regardless of how good one's ideas are. ■

Practical Exercises

Here are exercises relating to the application of ethics. Doing these will help increase your understanding of the subject.

1 Look around in your environment (your neighborhood, place of work, etc.) and find at least five examples of someone who has his ethics in. Then find five examples of someone who has his ethics out.

2 Look around your environment and locate an individual or activity which is in each of the following conditions: Non-Existence, Danger, Emergency, Normal, Affluence, Power. Do this until you are fully familiar with each condition as a state of existence.

3 Look around your environment and locate an individual or activity which is in a condition below Non-Existence. What condition is the person or activity in?

4 Using a separate sheet of paper, work out the statistic for some area of your life and show this on a graph. Determine what condition should be applied to that statistic.

5 Determine the condition of some aspect of your life, such as your job, your social life, your marriage, family life, anything. Once you have determined the correct condition, write down on a sheet of paper what you would do to apply each step of the formula for that condition.

6 Help someone you know determine the correct condition for a part of his or her life. When the correct condition has been established, show the person the formula for that condition and get the person to work out what he or she would do to apply that formula.

RESULTS FROM APPLICATION

Armed with the technology and tools of ethics developed by Mr. Hubbard, prosperity and a better life can be matters of certainty, not just chance or luck.

The use of ethics technology by the Director of the Juvenile Court in Greensville, Alabama, to deal with the problem of rehabilitating young criminals illustrates its workability. Statistics show that almost one for one, youngsters who embark on a life of crime remain criminals their entire lives. However, through use of Scientology ethics technology in counseling young offenders, this man achieved the unheard of: 90 percent of the youths he has counseled have not returned to prison after release. More than 500 testimonials have been written by those he has worked with, crediting ethics with having changed their lives forever.

In Greece, a man on trial for car theft was introduced to Scientology ethics. He put the data to use, made a clean breast of his crimes and made many outstanding contributions to the community as amends for his earlier misdeeds. When the man's attorney presented evidence of his reform and new value as a citizen, the judge on the case dismissed all charges.

Visiting her parents for the first time in a number of years, a young California woman was distressed to find that they were having problems with their marriage and were contemplating divorce. Rather than sit by and let that happen, she used what she knew of ethics technology.

"I spent time with my father going over the different conditions and their formulas, as well as basic Scientology data on creating and expanding a marriage. We established his correct condition with regard to the area and he applied its formula with great success. Next I spent time with my mother, working out how she could apply ethics to the difficulties she faced in the marriage. She realized that she had earlier given up on handling a financial problem with my father, and determined to resolve it. Once they began applying the ethics formulas, my parents' troubles were sorted out and their marriage became happier and more successful than it had been in many years."

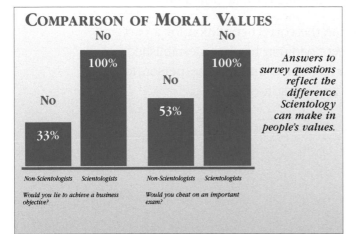

COMPARISON OF MORAL VALUES

	No		No
No	100%	No	100%
33%		53%	
Non-Scientologists	Scientologists	Non-Scientologists	Scientologists
Would you lie to achieve a business objective?		Would you cheat on an important exam?	

Answers to survey questions reflect the difference Scientology can make in people's values.

Being well versed in Scientology ethics, a community volunteer in South Africa was able to bring calm to an environment that had become turbulent after a series of unsolved thefts.

"I got into communication with the child who was suspected of stealing. Because I made it safe for her, she told me everything she had done. We worked out what she could do for the community to make up for the harm she had done, and she was happy about this. Because there had been so much upset about the thefts, I next assembled all the children (about seventy), and the young girl stood in front of the class and told them what she had done. I told the children that after the meeting there was to be no finger-pointing. They promised there wouldn't be any and officially forgave her. I was a little concerned about how the girl would feel after the meeting, but I found her playing happily with a group of children. I also found out that both the child's parents had been killed a few years earlier, and as she looked quite neglected I took measures to ensure she would be better looked after. The upset in the group was handled and the girl had a chance to become a true member of her group."

A man and his family opened a furniture business in Los Angeles; though they began with nothing, they achieved swift expansion by applying the conditions formulas.

"We studied and applied the data on conditions by Mr. Hubbard and began applying the Non-Existence Formula by the book. It was then that miracles started to happen. We opened up our communication lines and in the second month of operation two large loan companies offered us $50,000 in credit each. We got up into Danger and applied that formula, then Emergency and then Normal. We continued to apply the conditions by the book, achieving more expansion in one year than other businesses normally experience in fifteen years or more. We were even able to open a second store in our first year! Our expansion is stable through the application of the formulas."

The owner of a large restaurant chain uses Mr. Hubbard's data on conditions formulas to help his employees be honest and ethical.

"I had one employee who stole some money and another who allowed a great deal of money to be taken. Both were demoted, assigned the correct ethics condition and allowed to work their way back to executive positions through application of the conditions formulas. Now one of them is a successful franchise owner and the other is a key executive. Had it not been for the conditions formulas, I would have lost two valuable people."

GLOSSARY

acknowledge: give (someone) an acknowledgment. *See also* **acknowledgment** in this glossary.

acknowledgment: something said or done to inform another that his statement or action has been noted, understood and received.

beingness: condition or state of being; existence. *Beingness* also refers to the assumption or choosing of a category of identity. Beingness can be assumed by oneself or given to oneself or attained. Examples of beingness would be one's own name, one's profession, one's physical characteristics, one's role in a game—each or all of these could be called one's beingness.

bypass: jump the proper person in a chain of command.

communication: an interchange of ideas across space between two individuals.

communication line: the route along which a communication travels from one person to another.

condition: one of the states of operation or existence which an organization, its parts or an individual passes through. Each condition has an exact sequence of steps, called a formula, which one can use to move from the current condition to another higher and more survival condition.

determinism: power of choice; power of decision; ability to decide or determine the course of one's actions.

ethics: the actions an individual takes on himself to correct some conduct or situation in which he is involved which is contrary to the ideals and best interests of his group. It is a personal thing. When one is ethical or "has his ethics in," it is by his own determinism and is done by himself.

gradient: a gradual approach to something taken step by step, level by level, each step or level being, of itself, easily attainable—so that finally, complicated and difficult activities can be achieved with relative ease. The term *gradient* also applies to each of the steps taken in such an approach.

justice: the action taken on an individual by the group when he fails to take appropriate ethics actions himself.

Locational Processing: a type of process which helps orient a person and puts him in communication with his environment.

overt act: a harmful act or a transgression against the moral code of a group. An overt act is not just injuring someone or something, it is an act of *omission* or *commission* which does the least good for the least number of people or areas of life, or the most harm to the greatest number of people or areas of life.

processing: a special form of personal counseling, unique in Scientology, which helps an individual look at his own existence and improves his ability to confront what he is and where he is. Processing is a precise, thoroughly codified activity with exact procedures.

reality: agreement upon perceptions and data in the physical universe. All that we can be sure is real is that on which we have agreed is real. Agreement is the essence of reality.

Scientology: an applied religious philosophy developed by L. Ron Hubbard. It is the study and handling of the spirit in relationship to itself, universes and other life. The word *Scientology* comes from the Latin *scio*, which means "know" and the Greek word *logos*, meaning "the word or outward form by which the inward thought is expressed and made known." Thus, Scientology means knowing about knowing.

terminal: a person, point or position which can receive, relay or send a communication.

withhold: an unspoken, unannounced transgression against a moral code by which a person is bound; an overt act that a person committed that he or she is not talking about. Any withhold comes *after* an overt act.

ABOUT L. RON HUBBARD

Born in Tilden, Nebraska on March 13, 1911, his road of discovery and dedication to his fellows began at an early age. By the age of nineteen, he had traveled more than a quarter of a million miles, examining the cultures of Java, Japan, India and the Philippines.

Returning to the United States in 1929, Ron resumed his formal education and studied mathematics, engineering and the then new field of nuclear physics—all providing vital tools for continued research. To finance that research, Ron embarked upon a literary career in the early 1930s, and soon became one of the most widely read authors of popular fiction. Yet never losing sight of his primary goal, he continued his mainline research through extensive travel and expeditions.

With the advent of World War II, he entered the United States Navy as a lieutenant (junior grade) and served as commander of antisubmarine corvettes. Left partially blind and lame from injuries sustained during combat, he was diagnosed as permanently disabled by 1945. Through application of his theories on the mind, however, he was not only able to help fellow servicemen, but also to regain his own health.

After five more years of intensive research, Ron's discoveries were presented to the world in *Dianetics: The Modern Science of Mental Health.* The first popular handbook on the human mind expressly written for the man in the street, *Dianetics* ushered in a new era of hope for mankind and a new phase of life for its author. He did, however, not cease his research, and as breakthrough after breakthrough was carefully codified through late 1951, the applied religious philosophy of Scientology was born.

Because Scientology explains the whole of life, there is no aspect of man's existence that L. Ron Hubbard's subsequent work did not address. Residing variously in the United States and England, his continued research brought forth solutions to such social ills as declining educational standards and pandemic drug abuse.

All told, L. Ron Hubbard's works on Scientology and Dianetics total forty million words of recorded lectures, books and writings. Together, these constitute the legacy of a lifetime that ended on January 24, 1986. Yet the passing of L. Ron Hubbard in no way constituted an end; for with a hundred million of his books in circulation and millions of people daily applying his technologies for betterment, it can truly be said the world still has no greater friend. ■

CHURCHES OF SCIENTOLOGY

WESTERN UNITED STATES

Church of Scientology of Arizona
2111 W. University Dr.
Mesa, Arizona 85201

Church of Scientology of the Valley
3619 West Magnolia Boulevard
Burbank, California 91506

**Church of Scientology of
Los Angeles**
4810 Sunset Boulevard
Los Angeles, California 90027

**Church of Scientology of
Mountain View**
2483 Old Middlefield Way
Mountain View, California 96043

Church of Scientology of Pasadena
263 E. Colorado Boulevard
Pasadena, California 91101

**Church of Scientology of
Sacramento**
825 15th Street
Sacramento, California 95814

Church of Scientology of San Diego
635 "C" Street, Suite 200
San Diego, California 92101

**Church of Scientology of
San Francisco**
83 McAllister Street
San Francisco, California 94102

**Church of Scientology of
Stevens Creek**
80 E. Rosemary
San Jose, California 95112

**Church of Scientology of
Santa Barbara**
524 State Street
Santa Barbara, California 93101

**Church of Scientology of
Orange County**
1451 Irvine Boulevard
Tustin, California 92680

Church of Scientology of Colorado
375 S. Navajo Street
Denver, Colorado 80223

Church of Scientology of Hawaii
1146 Bethel Street
Honolulu, Hawaii 96813

Church of Scientology of Minnesota
Twin Cities
1011 Nicollet Mall
Minneapolis, Minnesota 55403

**Church of Scientology of
Kansas City**
3619 Broadway
Kansas City, Missouri 64111

Church of Scientology of Missouri
9510 Page Boulevard
St. Louis, Missouri 63132

Church of Scientology of Nevada
846 E. Sahara Avenue
Las Vegas, Nevada 89104

**Church of Scientology of
New Mexico**
8106 Menaul Boulevard N.E.
Albuquerque, New Mexico 87110

Church of Scientology of Portland
323 S.W. Washington
Portland, Oregon 97204

Church of Scientology of Texas
2200 Guadalupe
Austin, Texas 78705

Church of Scientology of Utah
1931 S. 1100 East
Salt Lake City, Utah 84106

**Church of Scientology of
Washington State**
2226 3rd Avenue
Seattle, Washington 98121

EASTERN UNITED STATES

Church of Scientology of Connecticut
909 Whalley Avenue
New Haven, Connecticut 06515

Church of Scientology of Florida
120 Giralda Avenue
Coral Gables, Florida 33134

Church of Scientology of Orlando
1830 East Colonial Drive
Orlando, Florida 32803

Church of Scientology of Tampa
3617 Henderson Boulevard
Tampa, Florida 33609

Church of Scientology of Georgia
2632 Piedmont Road, N.E.
Atlanta, Georgia 30324

Church of Scientology of Illinois
3011 N. Lincoln Avenue
Chicago, Illinois 60657

Church of Scientology of Boston
448 Beacon Street
Boston, Massachusetts 02115

Church of Scientology of Ann Arbor
2355 West Stadium Boulevard
Ann Arbor, Michigan 48103

Church of Scientology of Michigan
321 Williams Street
Royal Oak, Michigan 48067

Church of Scientology of Buffalo
47 West Huron Street
Buffalo, New York 14202

**Church of Scientology of
Long Island**
99 Railroad Station Plaza
Hicksville, New York 11801

Church of Scientology of New York
227 West 46th Street
New York City, New York 10036

Church of Scientology of Cincinnati
215 West 4th Street, 5th Floor
Cincinnati, Ohio 45202

Church of Scientology of Ohio
30 North High Street
Columbus, Ohio 43215

**Church of Scientology of
Pennsylvania**
1315 Race Street
Philadelphia, Pennsylvania 19107

**Founding Church of Scientology of
Washington, DC**
2125 "S" Street N.W.
Washington, DC 20008

PUERTO RICO

**Church of Scientology of
Puerto Rico**
272 JT Piniero Avenue
Hyde Park, Hato Rey
Puerto Rico 00918

UNITED KINGDOM

**Church of Scientology of
Birmingham**
Albert House, 3rd Floor
24 Albert Street
Birmingham
England B4 7UD

Church of Scientology of Brighton
5 St. Georges Place
London Road
Brighton, Sussex
England BN1 4GA

**Church of Scientology
Saint Hill Foundation**
Saint Hill Manor
East Grinstead, West Sussex
England RH19 4JY

Church of Scientology of London
68 Tottenham Court Road
London
England W1P 0BB

**Church of Scientology of
Manchester**
258 Deansgate
Manchester
England M3 4BG

Church of Scientology of Plymouth
41 Ebrington Street
Plymouth, Devon
England PL4 9AA

Church of Scientology of Sunderland
51 Fawcett Street
Sunderland, Tyne and Wear
England SR1 1RS

**Hubbard Academy of Personal
Independence**
20 Southbridge
Edinburgh
Scotland EH1 1LL

EUROPE

Austria

Church of Scientology of Austria
Schottenfeldgasse 13/15
1070 Wien

Belgium

Church of Scientology of Belgium
61, rue du Prince Royal
1050 Bruxelles

Denmark

Church of Scientology of Jylland
Guldsmedegade 17, 2
8000 Aarhus C

**Church of Scientology of
Copenhagen**
Store Kongensgade 55
1264 Copenhagen K

Church of Scientology of Denmark
Gammel Kongevej 3–5, 1
1610 Copenhagen V

France

Church of Scientology of Angers
10–12, rue Max Richard
49100 Angers

**Church of Scientology of
Clermont-Ferrand**
1, rue Ballainvilliers
63000 Clermont-Ferrand

Church of Scientology of Lyon
3, place des Capucins
69001 Lyon

Church of Scientology of Paris
65, rue de Dunkerque
75009 Paris

**Church of Scientology of
Saint-Étienne**
24, rue Marengo
42000 Saint-Étienne

Germany

Church of Scientology of Berlin
Sponholzstraße 51–52
12159 Berlin

Church of Scientology of Düsseldorf
Friedrichstraße 28
40217 Düsseldorf

Church of Scientology of Frankfurt
Darmstädter Landstraße 213
60598 Frankfurt

Church of Scientology of Hamburg
Steindamm 63
20099 Hamburg

Church of Scientology of Hanover
Hubertusstraße 2
30163 Hannover

Church of Scientology of Munich
Beichstraße 12
80802 München

Church of Scientology of Stuttgart
Urbanstraße 70
70182 Stuttgart

Israel
Dianetics and Scientology College
  of Israel
42 Gorden Street, 2nd Floor
Tel Aviv 66023

Italy
Church of Scientology of Brescia
Via Fratelli Bronzetti, 20
25125 Brescia

Church of Scientology of Catania
Via Garibaldi, 9
95121 Catania

Church of Scientology of Milan
Via Abetone, 10
20137 Milano

Church of Scientology of Monza
Via Cavour, 5
20052 Monza

Church of Scientology of Novara
Corso Cavallotti, 7
28100 Novara

Church of Scientology of Nuoro
Via Lamarmora, 115
08100 Nuoro

Church of Scientology of Padua
Via Mameli, 1/5
35131 Padova

Church of Scientology of Pordenone
Via Montereale, 10/C
33170 Pordenone

Church of Scientology of Rome
Via della Pineta Sacchetti, 201
00185 Roma

Church of Scientology of Turin
Via Bersezio, 7
10152 Torino

Church of Scientology of Verona
Via Vicolo Chiodo, 4/A
37121 Verona

Netherlands
Church of Scientology of Amsterdam
Nieuwe Zijds Voorburgwal 271
1012 RL Amsterdam

Norway
Church of Scientology of Norway
Storgata 9
0155 Oslo 1

Portugal
Church of Scientology of Portugal
Rua Actor Taborda 39–5°
1000 Lisboa

Russia
Hubbard Humanitarian Center
103064 Moscow
Homutovskiy Tupik 7, Russia

Spain
**Dianetics Civil Association of
  Barcelona**
C/ Pau Clarís 85, Principal dcha.
08010 Barcelona

**Dianetics Civil Association of
  Madrid**
C/ Montera 20, 1° dcha.
28013 Madrid

Sweden
Church of Scientology of Göteborg
Odinsgatan 8, 2 tr.
411 03 Göteborg

Church of Scientology of Malmö
Lantmannagatan 62 C
214 48 Malmö

Church of Scientology of Stockholm
St. Eriksgatan 56
112 34 Stockholm

Switzerland
Church of Scientology of Basel
Herrengrabenweg 56
4054 Basel

Church of Scientology of Bern
Dammweg 29
Postfach 352
3000 Bern 11

Church of Scientology of Geneva
Route de Saint-Julien 7–9 C.P. 823
1227 Carouge, Genève

Church of Scientology of Lausanne
10, rue de la Madeleine
1003 Lausanne

Church of Scientology of Zurich
Badenerstrasse 141
8004 Zürich

AFRICA

Church of Scientology of Cape Town
St. Georges Centre, 2nd Floor
13 Hout Street
Cape Town 8001
Republic of South Africa

Church of Scientology of Durban
57 College Lane
Durban 4001
Republic of South Africa

**Church of Scientology of
  Johannesburg**
Security Building, 2nd Floor
95 Commissioner Street
Johannesburg 2001
Republic of South Africa

**Church of Scientology of
  Johannesburg North**
1st Floor Bordeaux Centre
Gordon and Jan Smuts Ave.
Bordeaux, Randburg 2125
Republic of South Africa

**Church of Scientology of
  Port Elizabeth**
2 St. Christopher Place
27 Westbourne Road Central
Port Elizabeth 6001
Republic of South Africa

Church of Scientology of Pretoria
306 Ancore Building
Jeppe and Esselen Streets
Pretoria 0002
Republic of South Africa

Church of Scientology of Bulawayo
Southampton House, Suite 202
Main Street and 9th Avenue
Bulawayo, Zimbabwe

Church of Scientology of Harare
PO Box 3524
87 Livingston Road
Harare, Zimbabwe

AUSTRALIA, NEW ZEALAND AND OCEANIA

Australia
Church of Scientology of Adelaide
24–28 Waymouth Street
Adelaide, South Australia 5000

Church of Scientology of Brisbane
106 Edward Street
Brisbane, Queensland 4000

**Church of Scientology of
  Australian Capital Territory**
108 Bunda Street, Suite 16
Civic Canberra, A.C.T. 2601

Church of Scientology of Melbourne
42–44 Russell Street
Melbourne, Victoria 3000

Church of Scientology of Perth
39–41 King Street
Perth, Western Australia 6000

Church of Scientology of Sydney
201 Castlereagh Street
Sydney, New South Wales 2000

Japan
Scientology Tokyo
1-23-1 Higashi Gotanda
Shinagawa-ku
Tokyo, Japan 141

New Zealand
Church of Scientology New Zealand
32 Lorne Street
Auckland 1

LATIN AMERICA

Colombia
Dianetics Cultural Center
Calle 95 No. 19-A-28
Barrio Chico, Bogotá

Mexico
Dianetics Cultural Organization, A.C.
Pedro Moreno 1078 Int 3
Sector Juárez, Guadalajara, Jalisco

Dianetics Cultural Association, A.C.
Carrillo Puerto 54 Bis
Colonia Coyoacán
C.P. 04000, Mexico, D.F.

Latin American Cultural Center, A.C.
Durango 105
Colonia Roma
C.P. 03100, Mexico, D.F.

Institute of Applied Philosophy, A.C.
Juan de Dios Arias 83
Colonia Vista Alegre
Mexico, D.F.

Dianetics Technological Institute, A.C.
Avenida Juan Escutia 29
Colonia Condesa
Delegación Cuauhtemoc
C.P. 06140, Mexico, D.F.

Dianetics Development
  Organization, A.C.
Heriberto Frías 420
Colonia Narvarte
C.P. 03020, Mexico, D.F.

Dianetics Cultural Organization, A.C.
Nicolás San Juan 1734
Colonia del Valle
C.P. 03100, Mexico, D.F.

Venezuela
Dianetics Cultural Organization, A.C.
Avenida Principal de las Palmas,
  Cruce Con Calle Carúpano
Quinta Suha, Las Palmas
Caracas

Dianetics Cultural Association, A.C.
Avenida 101, 150-23
Urbanización La Alegría
Apartado Postal 833
Valencia

CANADA

Church of Scientology of Edmonton
10187 112th Street
Edmonton, Alberta
Canada T5K 1M1

Church of Scientology of Kitchener
104 King Street West
Kitchener, Ontario
Canada N2G 2K6

Church of Scientology of Montreal
4489 Papineau Street
Montréal, Québec
Canada H2H 1T7

Church of Scientology of Ottawa
150 Rideau Street, 2nd Floor
Ottawa, Ontario
Canada K1N 5X6

Church of Scientology of Quebec
350 Bd Chareste Est
Québec, Québec
Canada G1K 3H5

Church of Scientology of Toronto
696 Yonge Street, 2nd Floor
Toronto, Ontario
Canada M4Y 2A7

Church of Scientology of Vancouver
401 West Hasting Street
Vancouver, British Columbia
Canada V6B 1L5

Church of Scientology of Winnipeg
388 Donald Street, Suite 125
Winnipeg, Manitoba
Canada R3B 2J4

CELEBRITY CENTRES

**Church of Scientology
Celebrity Centre International**
5930 Franklin Avenue
Hollywood, California 90028

**Church of Scientology
Celebrity Centre Dallas**
10500 Steppington Drive, Suite 100
Dallas, Texas 75230

Bridge Publications, Inc.
4751 Fountain Ave., Los Angeles, CA 90029
ISBN 0-88404-917-5

NEW ERA Publications International ApS
Store Kongensgade 55, 1264 Copenhagen K, Denmark
ISBN 87-7816-109-6

An L. RON HUBBARD Publication

**Church of Scientology
Celebrity Centre Las Vegas**
1100 South 10th Street
Las Vegas, Nevada 89104

**Church of Scientology
Celebrity Centre Nashville**
38 Music Square West
Nashville, Tennessee 37203

**Church of Scientology
Celebrity Centre New York**
65 East 82nd Street
New York City, New York 10036

**Church of Scientology
Celebrity Centre Portland**
709 Southwest Salmon Street
Portland, Oregon 97205

**Church of Scientology
Celebrity Centre Washington, DC**
4214 16th Street N.W.
Washington, DC 20011

**Church of Scientology
Celebrity Centre London**
27 Westbourne Grove
London W2, England

**Church of Scientology
Celebrity Centre Vienna**
Senefeldergasse 11/5
1100 Wien, Austria

**Church of Scientology
Celebrity Centre Paris**
69, rue Legendre
75017 Paris, France

**Church of Scientology
Celebrity Centre Düsseldorf**
Grupellostraße 28
40210 Düsseldorf, Germany

**Church of Scientology
Celebrity Centre Hamburg**
Eppendorfer Landstraße 35
20249 Hamburg, Germany

**Church of Scientology
Celebrity Centre Munich**
Landshuter Allee 42
80637 München, Germany

SCIENTOLOGY MISSIONS

International Office

Scientology Missions International
6331 Hollywood Boulevard,
    Suite 501
Los Angeles, California 90028

▲ Scientology Missions International
Expansion Office
210 South Fort Harrison Avenue
Clearwater, Florida 34616

Western United States

▲ Scientology Missions International
Western United States Office
1307 N. New Hampshire,
    Suite 101
Los Angeles, California 90027

Eastern United States

▲ Scientology Missions International
Eastern United States Office
349 W. 48th Street
New York City, New York 10036

United Kingdom

▲ Scientology Missions International
United Kingdom Office
Saint Hill Manor
East Grinstead, West Sussex
England RH19 4JY

Europe

▲ Scientology Missions International
European Office
Store Kongensgade 55
1264 Copenhagen K
Denmark

Africa

▲ Scientology Missions International
African Office
Security Building, 2nd Floor
95 Commissioner Street
Johannesburg 2001
Republic of South Africa

Australia, New Zealand and Oceania

▲ Scientology Missions International
Australian, New Zealand and
    Oceanian Office
201 Castlereagh Street
Sydney, New South Wales 2000
Australia

Latin America

▲ Scientology Missions International
Latin American Office
Federación Mexicana de
    Dianética
Pomona 53
Colonia Roma
C.P. 06700, Mexico, D.F.

Canada

▲ Scientology Missions International
Canadian Office
696 Yonge Street
Toronto, Ontario
Canada M4Y 2A7

INTERNATIONAL HUBBARD ECCLESIASTICAL LEAGUE OF PASTORS

International Office

6331 Hollywood Boulevard, Suite 901
Los Angeles, California 90028
Telephone: 213-960-3560
US & Canada: 1-800-HELP-4-YU

Western United States

▲ Continental Liaison Office
Western United States
1307 N. New Hampshire
Los Angeles, California 90027

Eastern United States

▲ Continental Liaison Office
Eastern United States
349 W. 48th Street
New York City, New York 10036

United Kingdom

▲ Continental Liaison Office
United Kingdom
Saint Hill Manor
East Grinstead, West Sussex
England RH19 4JY

Canada

▲ Continental Liaison Office Canada
696 Yonge Street
Toronto, Ontario
Canada M4Y 2A7

Africa

▲ Continental Liaison Office Africa
Security Building, 4th Floor
95 Commissioner Street
Johannesburg 2001
Republic of South Africa

Latin America

▲ Continental Liaison Office
Latin America
Federación Mexicana de Dianética
Avenida Montevideo 486
Colonia Linda Vista
C.P. 07300
Mexico, D.F.

Australia, New Zealand and Oceania

▲ Continental Liaison Office ANZO
201 Castlereagh Street, 3rd Floor
Sydney, New South Wales 2000
Australia

Europe

▲ Continental Liaison Office Europe
Store Kongensgade 55
1264 Copenhagen K
Denmark